KŌRERO TAHI TALKING TOGETHER

KŌRERO TAHI TALKING TOGETHER

Joan Metge

Illustrations by Malcolm Evans

AUCKLAND UNIVERSITY PRESS
WITH TE MATAHAUARIKI INSTITUTE

First published 2001

Auckland University Press
University of Auckland
Private Bag 92019
Auckland
New Zealand
http://www.auckland.ac.nz/aup

© Joan Metge, 2001

Royalties to the Kotare Trust for Māori purposes

ISBN 1 86940 254 5

Cover design: Christine Hansen
Front cover illustration: Malcolm Evans

Printed by Printlink Ltd, Wellington

Dedicated to

HOANI RETIMANA WAITITI
Te Whānau-ā-Apanui
whose vision was the seed

and

DEREK ASHER (TE TAWIRI O TE RANGI MANUNUI)
Ngāti Tuwharetoa
who nurtured its growing

CONTENTS

FOREWORD

For the last five years I have been Director of Te Matahauariki Institute, a research group based within the School of Law at the University of Waikato, with a programme title 'Laws and Institutions of Aotearoa/New Zealand'.

Our programme seeks to contribute to an intellectual climate to realise a vision of socially inclusive laws and political and legal institutions in Aotearoa/New Zealand derived from two many-stranded traditions. Such laws and institutions must have sufficient flexibility and robustness to meet the future needs of the citizens of Aotearoa/New Zealand, as individuals and as members of collectivities.

As an integral part of the collaborative research process, we have regular meetings and informal contact with a group of distinguished New Zealanders who act as our Advisory Panel. This serves also to provide an auditing mechanism to maintain the programme's focus in such a broad field. The advisory group includes socio-legal scholars, academics, Maori scholars and key government officials.

In that regard, we are hugely privileged to have Dame Joan Metge as a revered member and advisor. With the wealth of her scholarship and experience, her profound knowledge of Te Ao Māori enhanced as it is by an enchanting deference and respect for Māori cultural traditions, Dame Joan is an exemplar for those whose vision it is to see Māori and Pākehā working together as equal partners for a common purpose: a noble cause for which she has devoted much of her life.

This beautiful and truly seminal book puts forward a practical mode of 'managing discussion' with the utilisation of alternative procedures incorporating many insights derived from the tikanga Māori.

Perhaps just as importantly, it offers us all 'a way of doing partnership as well as talking about it'.

Ko Dr. Dame Joan Metge
He whaea rangimarie, aroha, wairua pono.

Kia hora te marino
Kia papa pounamu te moana
Kia tere te kārohirohi

May the calm be widespread
May the sea glisten like the greenstone
And may the shimmer of summer dance across thy pathway.

M. J. A. (Mick) BROWN

HOANI WAITITI

TURNING VISION INTO PRACTICE

The seed is sown

One wintry night in 1961 I went with Hoani Waititi[1] to a public meeting in west Auckland to speak in support of the Māori Education Foundation, newly established to address the high percentage of young Māori leaving school without qualifications. As the Foundation's chief architect, Hoani insisted on its being a co-operative enterprise, involving Māori and Pākehā equally. (In this context, the word Pākehā is used as the counterpart of Māori, encompassing all non-Māori New Zealanders.)[2] Such a wastage of human potential (Hoani argued) affected the nation as a whole, not Māori alone, and all of us must contribute to the solution. Under his direction the organising committee was made up of equal numbers of Māori and Pākehā and so were the speaking teams sent out to spread the message. The Foundation's funds were drawn from both Māori and Pākehā sources, subsidised by the government.[3]

At that first meeting, Hoani invited me to speak first. After I had read a carefully prepared paper full of facts, figures and reasoned argument, he stood up and, noteless, told the story of his life. At every turn his account gave personal meaning to the abstract points I had made, hammering them home. Working in tandem for the first time, I was exhilarated by the way we complemented and took fire from each other.

That night I learnt a lesson I have never forgotten. Hoani argued that as Māori and Pākehā we are bound together in one nation by the Treaty of Waitangi and by our shared history. He made that argument live for me by demonstrating how rewarding it was to work together for a common purpose. When Māori and Pākehā respect and trust each other, recognising our differences, we achieve our goals more effectively than we could alone, learn much that enriches us and have a great deal of fun in the process. Despite the seriousness of the subject, we laughed a lot that night in west Auckland.

1

Hoani Waititi's vision of Māori and Pākehā working together as equal partners and his success in implementing it in the early days of the Māori Education Foundation were all the more remarkable because the official policy of assimilation was still largely in place, the Treaty of Waitangi was considered of marginal importance by the government and most Pākehā, and opportunities for Māori to manage their affairs and practise their cultural ways were confined to private space in homes and marae. Fortunately, Hoani was not alone in his vision. A similar spirit animated the Māori Leadership Conferences held mainly between 1959 and 1965, organised and sponsored jointly by Māori communities and the Departments of University Extension in Auckland and Wellington.[4]

Gains – and losses

In the 1970s and 1980s a new wave of articulate Māori leaders (including many 'graduates' of the Māori Education Foundation and Māori Leadership Conferences) mounted a challenge to Pākehā domination which, with support from sympathetic Pākehā, effected major changes in Māori–Pākehā relations. The Treaty of Waitangi was brought to national consciousness as our nation's founding document. The government recognised the validity of Māori grievances and embarked on the process of redress through the Waitangi Tribunal and direct negotiation. Pākehā generally became more aware and respectful of Māori culture and there was a significant increase in the number of Māori words used without translation as part of the general New Zealand vocabulary. Māori pioneered initiatives as self-managing service providers in education and health. Publication of the report *Puao-Te-Ata-Tu*[5] ushered in changes in the way government departments related to Māori. Government departments and other public institutions (such as schools and libraries) added Māori to their English names and signs, incorporated the Treaty of Waitangi into their mission statements, appointed Māori cultural advisers and commissioned Māori art works for display in public spaces. Other organisations, including churches, museums and art galleries, reformed their constitutions to give Māori rights of self-governance and access to power at the highest level. Recognition of Māori practices was built into several new laws.[6]

Yet, in spite of remarkable advances, Māori and Pākehā are still a long way from achieving Hoani Waititi's vision of partnership on a national scale. Over the last ten years ground has actually been lost in some areas, and promising developments have been stalled or sidetracked. Relations between Māori and Pākehā are not improved by the news media, whose practitioners tend to highlight tensions and conflicts, at the expense of stories of cooperation and achievement.

In the late 1980s and 1990s technological change demanding ever more advanced skills, coupled with economic restructuring and globalisation of the market economy, disadvantaged Māori as a group compared with Pākehā, so that once again the government is developing strategies designed to 'close the gaps' in education, employment and health. Although Pākehā generally use an increased range of Māori words, they do so with seriously restricted meanings, missing their full richness and contextual variation. Literary and artistic taonga (treasures) such as the haka and the koru are adopted as general icons with limited understanding of their significance and reapplied in ways that distort their original meaning and purpose.

Ironically, the increased national recognition and respect accorded Māori and Māori ways lead to misunderstanding and separation as often as they do to understanding and cooperation. Compensating for 150 years of domination, many articulate Māori insist on exclusive rights to practise and control the tikanga (right ways) inherited from their ancestors.[7] Unwilling to educate Pākehā in Māori ways themselves, they are nevertheless quick to rebuke them for insensitivity or mistakes, making no allowance for ignorance, anxiety or learning difficulties. Pākehā with a good understanding of Māori language and culture often hold back from pursuing their interest out of respect and sympathy for what Māori have suffered, while many who would like to learn more are put off by fear of rebuff.

Although it is now common for Māori cultural practices such as karanga, pōwhiri, karakia and the ritual lifting of tapu[8] to be included in the planning of public occasions, they are typically additions rather than an integral part of the proceedings, 'clip-ons' carried out by Māori according to tikanga and

3

in the Māori language. Some Māori speakers, mindful of the traditional value of arohanui ki te tangata (consideration for others), provide translations and explanations, but the majority insist on Māori only. As a result most non-Māori sit through such rituals without understanding and fail to appreciate either their symbolism or their psychological insight. Lack of understanding breeds boredom, resentment and impatience with Māori aspirations.

In other areas of common life, where Māori and Pākehā work together, whether on committees, councils, commissions and boards, or in recreational settings, it is usual to use procedures and language derived from the cultural tradition of the Pākehā majority. To meet the needs of changing times, public and private organisations repeatedly import concepts and processes from overseas – in the fields of family relations and restorative justice, for example – overlooking or discounting those that are alive and well in our own country in the Māori community. Although there is greater recognition of their right to manage themselves and their own affairs, Māori are still expected to conform to the majority pattern, to cope with moving between two cultural worlds where Pākehā generally live comfortably in one.

Understanding the Treaty

Part of the problem has its roots in continuing arguments over interpretation of the Treaty of Waitangi. These arguments arise when commentators focus on particular aspects of the Treaty at the expense of others: on the English text without reference to the Māori, on the Māori text without reference to the English, or on only one of the three articles. Because of the difficulty of translating British legal concepts into Māori, there are significant differences between the English text (identified as *the* Treaty by most Pākehā) and the Māori text, which was read to and signed by the Māori signatories, few of whom understood English.[9] The three articles are not alternatives but complement and build on each other. To understand the spirit of the Treaty, it is important to consider it as a whole that is greater than the sum of its parts. As such, it is a covenant agreement by which two peoples committed themselves to forming one nation, living and working together in peace, justice and interdependence. Moreover, it is a continuing covenant, passed on from generation to generation of New Zealand citizens, encompassing all who have been integrated into the nation after settling here, as well as the descendants of Treaty signatories.

Under the Treaty, it is right and proper that Māori be supported in pursuing and developing their ancestral tikanga in their own way and spaces, but it is also essential that Māori and Pākehā (using that term in its widest sense)[10] work together as partners to create a national life, a national culture, to which all contribute, in which all feel they have a share, with which all feel comfortable. Revising the constitution may go some way to achieving this but it will be ineffective unless accompanied or, preferably, preceded by changes in practice. If we are to realise the vision of partnership implicit in the Treaty, we need more effective communication, more sharing, more cross-fertilisation in our public life, as well as mutual recognition of rights. In particular, we need to recognise the value of drawing on the Māori as well as the European cultural tradition as a source of inspiration for our common culture.

Managing discussion

An area of particular importance for cross-cultural communication and cooperation is that of group discussion, whether it is aimed at exploring a subject or coming to a decision. At present, when people of different ethnic backgrounds meet in discussion, it is usual to use only the English language and the rules familiar to the Pākehā majority. As a result, members of minority groups often feel at a disadvantage, fail to contribute to their full capacity or become aggressively assertive. We need a procedure that is acceptable and enjoyable to all.

Māori long ago borrowed committee procedure from Pākehā, applied it to the management of business meetings and subtly changed it in the process, but Pākehā have generally failed to recognise the values and rules governing discussion in Māori settings as a source worth tapping. They have remained monocultural in this context and have imposed their monocultural practice on Māori. Ethnocentricity aside, this has happened partly because the tikanga governing discussion on the marae are not codified and available in packaged form; instead, Māori internalise them in the process of growing up in Māori communities, learning by doing. Once these tikanga are brought to consciousness, it is clear that they are rooted in a deep understanding of human psychology. When applied by skilled practitioners, they are highly effective in achieving their aims. They are a resource Pākehā have been foolish to neglect.

This book draws on that rich resource to develop a procedure for managing group discussion in general settings where Māori from many iwi and Pākehā from many ethnic groups meet to talk about common concerns. I have named this procedure kōrero tahi – talking together, the opposite of talking past each other.[11]

Kōrero tahi procedure aims to create an environment that is comfortable and empowering to *all* participants in a discussion, an environment where none feel disadvantaged or intimidated by rules, words or actions they do not understand, and where all are accorded equal dignity and respect. To achieve this aim, discussion organisers must spell out the rules of kōrero tahi, explain its source and purposes and act as facilitators, not directors.

The rules of kōrero tahi balance rights with responsibilities. They guarantee participants the right to express themselves in the language of their choice – but require them to provide a translation or paraphrase for the benefit of those who do not understand the chosen language. Kōrero tahi encourages participants to air grievances and hostile feelings – but also to accept mediation and negotiate settlement. And, finally, kōrero tahi requires participants to leave behind what was negative in the discussion, taking away only what is constructive.

Respecting the Māori source

As a minority group with a long history of resisting assimilation, Māori are understandably sensitive to the threat of having their cultural taonga appropriated,[12] taken over by outsiders without authority, but they have been more than generous in sharing them with Pākehā who have proved themselves respectful and worthy of trust. Because Māori are justified in fearing appropriation, it needs to be emphasised that kōrero tahi has been developed *with* authority and under Māori guidance. It is based on five decades of observation in Māori settings, lengthy discussions with Māori experts on the subject, and cooperation with Māori partners in workshops designed to teach non-Māori about Māori ways of thinking and acting. In particular I acknowledge my debt to Hoani Waititi (Te Whānau-ā-Apanui), Matiu Te Hau (Whakatōhea and Ngā Puhi), Wiremu Parker (Ngāti Porou), Tawhao Tioke (Tūhoe), Derek Asher (Tūwharetoa), Keri Kaa (Ngāti Porou), Haami Piripi (Te Rarawa) and Tukaki Waititi (Whānau-ā-Apanui and Ngāti Hine of Ngā Puhi). These experts in tikanga Māori all contributed to and approved the development of kōrero tahi at different stages. Those still living (the last five named) have given their approval and support to its presentation in this work, including the choice of name.

To continue the pattern of cross-cultural cooperation thus established, those who use kōrero tahi procedure are asked to adopt four guiding principles:

- to acknowledge the Māori cultural tradition as the source and inspiration of kōrero tahi;
- to work to extend their own understanding of tikanga Māori as those tikanga operate in Māori contexts;
- to involve both Māori and Pākehā in any adaptation of the tikanga governing discussion for use in general settings;
- to arrange whenever possible for Māori and Pākehā to work together in partnership as organisers and facilitators.

As a way of managing group discussion, kōrero tahi is at once rooted in Aotearoa New Zealand and available for general use in a variety of settings. It is intended not to displace but to widen the options available to New Zealanders, recognising and catering for cultural diversity.

In each of the following sections, in the spirit of the above principles, I first set out the values, rules and practices of the Māori way of managing discussion, and then I do the same for kōrero tahi, showing how those Māori values, rules and practices (the Māori pattern) can be adapted for use in a wide variety of general situations, public and private.

First, a note on use of the shorthand phrase, the Māori pattern. In Māori contexts, members of different iwi insist on the independent identity of each, emphasising (even exaggerating) differences in dialect and tikanga. From a wider perspective, however, these differences appear as essentially variations on basic themes that are common to and valued by all who identify as Māori. The division into and structure of iwi is itself one of these basic themes. Others are the Māori language, the institution of the marae and the set of tikanga governing discussion, which are closely associated with the marae. For the purposes of this work, it is appropriate to focus primarily on the Māori pattern common to all iwi. The existence of tribal variations will, however, be noted where relevant.

SETTINGS, RULES AND THE USE OF SPACE

The Māori pattern

Māori collectively see the marae as the appropriate venue for debating issues of all kinds, especially at family and community level. Discussion is an integral part of every gathering held on a marae, whether the community is meeting on its own or entertaining visitors, and whatever the publicly announced reason for coming together. When Māori meet for discussion in other places, they transform them into the likeness of a marae by their use of space and application of marae rules of debate.

Discussion is so closely associated with the marae that the rules used in its management are commonly referred to in English as marae procedure, in

conscious opposition to committee procedure derived from Pākehā sources. This description is not completely accurate. Marae procedure in Māori is ngā tikanga o te marae, a phrase that covers *all* aspects of marae protocol, including behaviour in the kitchen and toilets as well as on the marae and in the meeting house. In Māori the rules governing discussion are properly identified as ngā tikanga kōrerorero.[13]

The rules for discussion in Māori settings are not hard-and-fast directives (though the inexperienced are tempted to treat them as such) but flexible guidelines that both encourage and require modification according to circumstances. In particular, they are modified according to whether the gathering is held on or off a marae complex, whether visitors are present or not and whether those visitors are kin or strangers. Like all tikanga Māori, they are grounded in basic Māori values, laying particular emphasis on respect for the spiritual dimension (expressed in karakia and the observance of tapu), ancestral connections (expressed in whakapapa and whanaungatanga), attachment to the land (whenua), generosity (aroha) and care for others (manaaki ki te tangata), peace (rangimārie) and unity (kotahitanga).

9

They are neither set out as a code nor formally taught: they are absorbed by watching and doing.

Among tikanga of varying levels of specificity, five are of basic importance:

- the use of physical space to express and mediate social relationships;
- the making of a distinction between tāngata whenua (the people of the land) and manuwhiri (visitors from elsewhere);[14]
- the framing of discussion with karakia (prayers invoking the spiritual dimension) and with ceremonials of greeting and farewell;
- the vesting of responsibility for the management of discussion in participants as a group;
- the appropriate use of one, two or three distinct modes of discussion.

Ngā tikanga kōrerorero are applied, by judicious selection and adaptation, to a variety of purposes. They may be used, on the same or different occasions, for exploring issues, making decisions, resolving disputes, investigating wrongdoing and restoring damaged relationships and social order.

Māori discussion processes are clearly shaped by and for the spaces available on a marae complex: the open space between gateway and meeting house (the marae ātea), the interior of the meeting house and the dining hall. When meeting on their own, without visitors, the people of a marae commonly hold formal, serious discussions in the meeting house and business meetings in the dining hall. When visitors arrive, they are welcomed either on the marae ātea or inside the meeting house, depending on the weather and tribal protocol. These spaces are also used for the discussions in which both hosts and visitors participate, but the hosts discuss operational matters privately in dining hall or kitchen.

Both marae ātea and meeting house consist of an open central space with seating at the sides. When visitors are being welcomed, the people of the marae (the hosts) occupy seats on one side, the visitors occupy the seats opposite and the two parties exchange speeches with each other across the space between.[15] Once the welcome is over, this initial separation into two groups is obliterated as hosts and visitors mix and mingle. Thereafter, those who wish to listen to or take part in public discussion remain together in one place, on the marae or inside the meeting house, as the hosts decide. In both cases, they seat themselves around a central space, which becomes the arena for speakers.

Adapting the Māori pattern for general settings

Outside Māori settings, Māori and non-Māori engage in formal discussion in a wide variety of contexts: in special interest conferences and workshops, in study courses and in the meetings of boards, councils and committees; in gatherings involving small to large numbers of participants; in single, one-off gatherings and in linked sequences of meetings. Depending on the number of participants and the time allowed, these discussions are held in a variety of venues: in small, intimate rooms, in more formal board and council rooms, in assembly halls and in convention centres containing several of these. Before deciding to use kōrero tahi procedure in any of these contexts, consideration has to be given to its underlying principles and rules and to the purposes for which they are suited.

Drawing on ngā tikanga kōrerorero, kōrero tahi procedure emphasises the following key principles:

- the organisation of space and seating in ways that make participants feel welcomed and included;
- explicit recognition of a distinction between organisers and other participants, or of the absence of such a distinction, as appropriate;
- the framing of discussion between semi-formal expressions of welcome and farewell;
- acceptance by all participants of collective responsibility for managing discussion;
- the complementary use of two to three modes of discussion.

Like ngā tikanga kōrerorero, kōrero tahi procedure can be used for a variety of purposes. It is ideally suited to discussions designed to explore a subject, a line of argument or a set of ideas without reaching conclusions, and/or to help people who work together to get to know and trust each

11

other, exposing underlying tensions so that they can be dealt with. As long as time is not limited, kōrero tahi is also effective in discussions oriented to the making of decisions or recommendations: for example, in the development of policies and action programmes, in the investigation of wrongdoing and the administration of restorative justice, and in the resolution of conflict.

Kōrero tahi procedure is, however, neither effective nor appropriate when discussing business and commercial matters nor when information has to be transferred to large numbers of recipients within tight time limits.

Business and commercial discussion is more appropriately handled by committee procedure and the transfer of information to many recipients is better managed by one presiding lecturer or chairperson.

At times, kōrero tahi may be the only procedure used, for example, in the management of gatherings designed to help a relatively small number of participants get to know each other and/or to share knowledge, experience and understanding in specialised fields. In many cases, however, kōrero tahi is appropriately used for selected sessions only: for example, in conducting workshops during courses and conferences which also use the lecture or plenary format, or when members of boards, councils and committees take time out from business matters to discuss policy and goals, to build team spirit and/or to deal with internal tensions. For examples of the adaptation of kōrero tahi for use in different situations, see pp.14 and 15.

Except when they take place at a marae, gatherings involving Māori and Pākehā are held in settings designed for Pākeha ways of handling discussion. Rows of seats are set out in one or more blocks facing a few chairs on a platform or behind a table, or chairs are set out around one or more tables. At first sight these settings are the very antithesis of that required by kōrero tahi procedure, which draws on the Māori pattern, but with imagination and the cooperation of participants they can usually be rearranged to suit.

For the welcome and plenary sessions at large-scale gatherings, the chairs on the platform or at the end of the room furthest from the door can be set out in two or three rows for the use of the organisers of the gathering (the 'hosts'), while the main body of the seating is allocated to those who attend at the organisers' invitation (the 'visitors').

In the case of small gatherings and conference workshops, participants may redefine the chairs-and-table combination as a round table; they may move the table out of the way and set the chairs in a circle around a central empty space; or they may dispense with furniture altogether to sit in a circle on the floor or on the grass under the trees.

13

KŌRERO TAHI IN A CONFERENCE CONTEXT

Early in 2000, the executive of a nationwide organisation invited me to introduce kōrero tahi procedure to delegates attending an annual conference, working in partnership with the organisation's Māori cultural adviser. We were allocated an afternoon session lasting three and a half hours.

Well before the conference, the adviser and I had two meetings at which we got to know each other and worked out our plan of campaign.

The conference was held in the conference facility of a city hotel. The adviser attended the conference from the beginning and played a leading part in organising a welcome ceremony for the delegates on arrival. He also arranged a small-scale welcome for me when I arrived just before lunch on the day our session was scheduled. The tables in the hotel's conference room were pushed aside to create just enough space for the purpose. One of the delegates welcomed me in Māori and English; the adviser replied in Māori and English on my behalf, according to the protocol of his iwi, where speaking in the welcome ceremony is a male responsibility. I shook hands with all the delegates in turn and we adjourned to the hotel dining room for lunch.

In the conference room after lunch the adviser and I worked together in dialogue, explaining the aims of kōrero tahi, the relevance of the Māori values and practices on which it draws for inspiration, and the general rules of the procedure to be used. After time for questions, the delegates sorted themselves into two groups, pushing aside more tables to make room for two circles of chairs. The adviser sat in one group and I sat in the other, and the executive officers distributed themselves between the two. We began by going round the circle, each delegate introducing themselves and laying down a work-related concern they wanted to discuss. These concerns were then discussed using criss-cross exchange. The delegates in my group had no difficulty in picking up and using the rules to advantage, even when the discussion became heated and produced tears. Discussion in the other group was equally lively but one delegate got carried away and had to be asked to stop. The delegates delayed afternoon tea so that they could conclude their discussions.

After the break the chairs were formed into a single circle and delegates passed a portable microphone backwards and forwards as a substitute stick, sharing the fruit of their discussion and suggesting steps that could be taken. When time was nearly up, the microphone came my way. I took the opportunity to make my farewells and passed it to the adviser, who summed up the afternoon's discussion and learning, thanked the executive for arranging the session and bade me farewell on the group's behalf.

KŌRERO TAHI IN A MARAE SETTING

Late in 1999 the Māori staff of a large northern secondary school invited me to work with them in planning and running a noho marae (overnight stay on a marae) for other staff members.

The process began with an exploratory meeting between myself and four Māori staff members, including the head of department for Māori studies, at which it was decided to adopt the kōrero tahi approach. Next came a two-hour meeting with eight Māori staff members at which I outlined the procedure and we used it to discuss the organisation of the noho marae. This allowed the Māori teachers to make the procedure their own and prepared them to serve as facilitators during the noho marae.

When the college staff gathered at the appointed marae at 5 p.m. one Friday night, they were called on to the marae and into the meeting house by one of the local kuia. Seated in the meeting house, they were welcomed by three tangata whenua speakers supported by a host group that included the deputy principal of the college (because he had ancestral connection with the marae), the head of department for Māori studies (a member of the marae community through marriage) and me (because of years of involvement in the community).

After the meal that followed the welcome, the participants gathered in the meeting house for an initial plenary session conducted by the deputy principal and me working as partners. We clarified the purpose of the noho marae, walked the visitors through the welcome ceremony so that they understood the significance of what had been said and done, including the reasons why two staff members sat with the tāngata whenua, set out the tikanga governing behaviour on the marae and outlined the procedure to be followed in discussion sessions. Then the participants divided themselves into five groups, each including two facilitators (all, except me, Māori staff members). Meeting either in the meeting house or dining room, these small groups began by going round the circle to lay down the topics they wanted discussed and then explored them using criss-cross exchange. The discussions were so lively that supper was delayed until 11 p.m.

Next morning we spent an hour together in a plenary session, sitting in the sun listening to the tāngata whenua explain the artwork and history of the marae and the surrounding area, then we resumed discussion in our small groups. After a late morning tea we returned to the meeting house for a plenary session in which we shared the fruits of our small group discussions, using a leafy branch as our talking stick, and concluded with a farewell session in time for a late lunch.

ORGANISATION AND LEADERSHIP

The Māori pattern

Whether they gather for discussion or other purposes, Māori make a basic distinction between tāngata whenua and manuwhiri, hosts and visitors. Under normal circumstances, the tāngata whenua are the hapū or whānau with ancestral rights in the locality where the gathering takes place, especially when it is held on a marae, and all others are visitors.

During a hui on their marae, the tāngata whenua are totally responsible for organising the proceedings. They welcome the visitors, initiate the stages in proper sequence, decide on the appropriate tikanga and deal with any problems that arise. It is their prerogative to invite others to join them in these tasks. If an outside organisation (such as the Waitangi Tribunal) arranges to hold a meeting on a marae, the tāngata whenua welcome its representatives as manuwhiri and then hand over to them the right to manage the meeting. If a gathering is held in a setting other than a marae, the organisers act as hosts but if they are not themselves tāngata whenua they often invite representatives of the latter to play a leading part in the welcome.

For their part, the visitors also have rights and responsibilities, notably the right to be treated with respect and hospitality during their visit and the responsibility to accept their hosts' lead, to contribute to the discussion and other activities, and to express their appreciation appropriately in words and action, including the giving of koha (gifts).

At Māori gatherings, whether on or off the marae, no one person is unequivocally in charge. Leadership and responsibility inhere in the group as a whole (whether hosts or visitors) and are delegated to a core of chosen representatives. Leading roles (plural) are filled by men and women who combine seniority of age and descent with competence as speakers and organisers. One or two may be particularly prominent, but they rely on the support and cooperation of others. They are team leaders rather than dictators.

In particular, male and female leaders work in close partnership, fulfilling complementary roles. This is equally true of those who work out the front, filling roles as kai-karanga (callers) and kai-kōrero (speakers), and those who work out the back, providing visitors with food and other comforts. In many activities men and women work together, for example, in singing waiata to complement speeches or preparing vegetables and washing dishes in the kitchen. In the event of conflict or offence, the older folk, especially the women, take on special roles as mediators and peacemakers. The person most prominent in action is not necessarily the most respected and influential: according to tradition, the most high-ranking tangata whenua speaks least and last, listening to others and summing up the consensus reached. All participants, whatever their status, are expected to exercise a degree of responsibility and self-discipline, holding back rather than pushing themselves forward, watching others to identify their needs and concerns, responding to non-verbal cues.

During hui, discussion takes place in plenary sessions in one place: on the marae, in the meeting house or in a private home, as the tangata whenua decide. Although the rules governing discussion in Māori settings are basically the same, there is some variation in their application according to the hosts' iwi affiliation, the setting chosen and whether visitors are present or not. On the open marae and in the meeting house, and when visitors are present, proceedings are conducted with greater formality, and participation is more likely to be restricted to speakers from certain categories, especially kaumātua (of both sexes) and the chosen representatives of whānau and hapū. When visitors are not present, and at certain times during hui (when a kaumātua 'opens it up', in the evenings, and on the last night of mourning before burial of the dead), those not old or experienced enough to fill representative roles are encouraged to have their say.

Finally, the discussion itself may be ordered in one or more of three ways: huri haere i te whare (going round the house), whakawhitiwhiti kōrero (open, criss-cross exchange) and te haere o te rākau (passing the stick). These three forms are typically used at different times and for different purposes, and are favoured to varying degrees by different iwi. Huri haere i te whare is generally used first, to enable people to introduce themselves and break the ice. Whakawhitiwhiti kōrero is used the most, for discussions of major import. Te haere o te rākau is used in the evenings, to involve the diffident and create a relaxed atmosphere.

Adapting the Māori pattern for general settings

In adapting the Māori pattern of organisation and leadership for general settings, adjustments must be made according to the size and composition of the group to be managed, the frequency with which the participants meet and the purposes they have in mind.

In the case of boards, councils, committees and comparable bodies, the host/visitor distinction is relevant only at the first meeting of a new term of service, when office-holders and members from the previous term appropriately extend a welcome to the newly elected or appointed. At subsequent meetings, all are equally members of the core community, the home folks. As on the marae, the absence of visitors emphasises members' community of interests, their responsibility to seek the common good and the importance of getting to know and trust each other.

In the organising of courses and conferences, a small band of workers, usually officials of the organisation or institution sponsoring the gathering, are readily identified as hosts. They invite the other participants, choose the venue, arrange meals and accommodation, assemble the programme and do what has to be done to make sure everything runs smoothly. As hosts applying kōrero tahi procedure, they also stage and take the lead in a formal welcome ceremony, which gets the gathering off to a good start by making participants feel both welcome and welcomed.

If members of the host group are familiar with kōrero tahi procedure, they can handle its introduction and conduct themselves; if not, they should pass the responsibility on to facilitators with the necessary experience. If such people are brought in from outside, the organisers should lead the participants who have already been welcomed in staging a short welcome in which they hand over to the facilitators the authority to manage the kōrero tahi sessions.

Depending on the size of the group and the availability of skilled personnel, the task of facilitating discussion may be carried out by two people working as a couple or by several working as a team. If possible, the couple or team should include both men and women, Māori and Pākehā, and people from older and younger age groups. The facilitators impart more

19

about the collective responsibility and cooperation at the heart of kōrero tahi by demonstrating it than by talking *about* it.

In preparing to use kōrero tahi, it is important that organisers and facilitators use the procedure themselves in their planning sessions, to discuss and develop a clear understanding of its aims, principles and implementation. By using it themselves they can explore its advantages and disadvantages and learn what it can and cannot be expected to achieve. They should also think out contingency plans for coping with crises such as rule-breaking and disruptive behaviour. In using the process together they will develop the ability to communicate non-verbally as well as verbally during discussion sessions. They will learn the importance of accepting the support of other participants, especially those senior to them in age and experience, in handling conflict and rule breaches, and they will come to appreciate the value and uses of silence.

The principle of collective, shared responsibility is of paramount importance in kōrero tahi. Instead of relying on one person with authority to maintain order and control rule-breaking, kōrero tahi places the responsibility squarely on the shoulders of *all* participants, hosts and visitors alike. Everyone must contribute to the success of the discussion by sharing their knowledge, experience and feelings, by disciplining themselves to give each other space literally and metaphorically, by supporting rather than undermining each other and by being prepared to challenge each other when necessary. Before embarking on the use of kōrero tahi, organisers are wise to explain this clearly and to take all the time needed to enlist participants' co-operation.

In contrast with Māori practice, which keeps participants together in one body, kōrero tahi advocates dividing them into small groups for at least part of the time available when their number rises above fifteen to twenty. Keeping a large group together reduces the opportunities for speaking and increases the risk of people becoming bored or inhibited by the number or identity of those listening. Division into small groups makes sure everyone is actively involved. Kōrero tahi treats plenary and small group discussions as complementary, using plenary sessions at the beginning to explain aims and general rules and at intervals and/or at the end to allow small groups to share their experience with each other.

Kōrero tahi makes use of all three Māori discussion modes by linking them into a sequence that capitalises on their respective strengths. This sequence may be used for one or more of several purposes: for exploring a subject, team-building, deciding on policy or courses of action, investigating and deciding what to do about wrongdoing and resolving conflict.

Now for details of the practical application of kōrero tahi in real-life situations.

GETTING OFF TO A GOOD START

The Māori pattern: the pōwhiri

When Māori from different groups or institutions gather, they begin proceedings with a formal ritual of encounter – the welcome ceremony known most widely as the pōwhiri.[16] Far from being the empty ritual assumed by those who do not understand Māori, the welcome ceremony is specifically designed to introduce individuals and groups to each other, reducing feelings of strangeness, anxiety or hostility to manageable proportions, so that everyone involved feels comfortable enough to engage in the real work of discussion to follow.

To this end, the pōwhiri begins by stressing the distance, literal and metaphorical, between the hosts and visitors and then brings them closer, literally and metaphorically, by successive stages. These stages involve a series of exchanges, initiated by the hosts and responded to by the visitors. The women's voices are heard first in an exchange of karanga (calling), the challenge by a tangata whenua warrior is answered by an action signifying peaceful intent by the visitors' leader, hosts and visitors join in shared remembrance of their dead, sit opposite each other to exchange speeches of greeting,[17] and, finally, make physical contact, hand to hand in the handshake, and nose to nose in the hongi – expressions of trust from different cultural sources. When this point is reached, the two parties break ranks to mingle with each other, and the ceremony is completed by sharing food and drink.

In word and action during the welcome ceremony, participants recognise the presence of spiritual beings and seek spiritual blessings on the gathering. This is done in various ways, implicitly as well as explicitly – in the karanga, in speeches, in waiata (songs) and in karakia (prayers). Where the karakia is placed varies between iwi: some place it before the speeches, some afterwards.

Adapting the pōwhiri for general settings

The pōwhiri as such can be mounted only by Māori for guests who understand and accept Māori leadership and management, but Māori and non-Māori working together may draw on its underlying insights to devise introductory welcome ceremonies for mixed or non-Māori settings, provided they acknowledge their source of inspiration.

A formal welcome ceremony is an idea worth borrowing, especially for situations where most participants do not know each other well and/or are entering unknown territory. It creates a pause between the outside world and the discussion, giving participants time to reorient themselves to the setting and purpose of the gathering and to become familiar with new faces. Its principal aim is to create a friendly, comfortable and safe environment that allays participants' anxieties, so that they can relax and open up.

Planning the welcome ceremony is both the prerogative and the responsibility of the organisers acting as hosts. They should begin planning it early, not leave it to the last minute, because it will set the tone of the gathering. They need to take account of the parties attending (with special reference

23

to age, ethnicity and interrelations), the numbers involved, the nature of the venue and any likely cultural sensitivities.

The first decision is who will rank as hosts and who will be accounted visitors. Besides the organisers, the hosts should include representatives of the gathering's sponsors and local residents, especially the tāngata whenua of the area.

Once that decision is made, the organisers must decide whether to ask the tāngata whenua to provide a pōwhiri or to devise a welcome ceremony modelled on the pōwhiri but not a reproduction of it. If the former course is followed (and it must be if the gathering is held on a marae), it must be accepted that the speeches will be mainly or entirely in Māori and will not be understood by many of those present. If the purposes of a welcome ceremony are to be achieved, the organisers must think about providing English translations or summaries of the speeches either during or after the pōwhiri. This used to be common on marae and in such situations as Māori Land Court sittings when Pākehā were present, but the practice has fallen out of favour in the drive to extend use of the Māori language.

For venues other than a marae, it would be in the spirit of kōrero tahi to design a welcome ceremony that uses the English language but also recognises the status of Māori as an official language and the presence of speakers of other languages. For example, the Māori language could be used to begin and end the ceremony with karanga and karakia, in the first speech and in waiata, while speakers from minority groups could be invited to use their own languages in speeches and songs, provided they explained the content in English. The important thing is that decisions of this kind are taken by Māori and Pākehā organisers working through the issues together.

Since a welcome ceremony – as distinct from 'a few words of welcome' – is not usual outside Māori circles, the organisers are advised to arrange for one or two facilitators to identify the elements of the ceremony and explain its underlying rationale. This may be done in a handout provided beforehand or in a last-minute briefing, so that participants are prepared for what follows. Or it may be done after the welcome, in the first plenary session, by eliciting from participants what they saw and understood, and filling in the gaps.

Here are some suggestions for developing a welcome ceremony modelled on the pōwhiri.

- In preparation for the arrival of the main body of participants, the organisers arrange the seats in two banks facing each other with a space between, preferably on the same level. Depending on circumstances, the two banks may be unequal in size, with relatively few seats on the hosts' side and many on the visitors'.
- As participants assemble, the organisers direct those classed as hosts to occupy one bank of seats and the visitors to occupy the other. If the venue allows, they may arrange for the visitors to gather outside the space where the seats are set out and formally invite them to come and take their seats as a body.
- Once everyone is in place, one or two host speakers welcome the visitors and one or two of the visitors reply. The two parties select the speakers to represent them and decide on the speaking order beforehand; they also settle what language or mix of languages will be used. Speakers should be advised to keep their speeches short, limiting them to greetings and the provision of necessary information about who is present and why they have come.
- At the conclusion of the speeches, the hosts' chief speaker invites the visitors to leave their seats and exchange individual personal greetings with the hosts and each other.
- Hosts and visitors mix in the sharing of a cup of tea or a meal. Sharing food provides relaxation after tension, extends the symbolism of sharing and allows individual interaction.
- An alternative format modelled on the flower ceremony of Te Tai Tokerau is set out on pp.27 and 28.
- Organisers should feel free to develop their own creative ideas.

Planners should consider whether to include a prayer for spiritual guidance and blessing, taking account of the likely beliefs and attitudes of participants. In a gathering that includes both Māori and Pākehā, insisting on a spiritual invocation can be divisive, defeating one of the main purposes of kōrero tahi. A frequent solution is to invite a Māori participant to say karakia in Māori, in the expectation that listeners will not be offended by what they cannot understand, but this sidesteps the issue. What is needed is an activity everyone can share, stressing togetherness. Singing a song together is one possibility. Or a leading host might invite participants to keep silence for a short time, focusing their minds on the importance of the coming discussion. Those who wish may then pray silently.

In the case of large, one-off gatherings, the hosts will have to make a decision on this point and be prepared to defend it. Where participants meet regularly, as on boards, councils and committees, the best solution is to discuss the issue openly (using kōrero tahi, of course!), exploring people's reasons for and against and developing a procedure acceptable to all. In this connection, it is helpful to explore the reasons Māori give for saying karakia: to remind participants of the importance of the spiritual as well as the physical dimension of human existence, to place them under tapu, set apart for a particular purpose under divine guidance, and to bind them together in assent to common values.

Hosts and visitors alike should constantly remind themselves of the purpose of the welcome ceremony, never forgetting that it is the prologue to the real business of the gathering: discussion. On the marae it is not tika (correct) to limit the number of speakers or ask speakers to speak briefly, but in this context it is strongly advised, to avoid encroaching on discussion time.

AN ALTERNATIVE WELCOME CEREMONY

The flower ceremony

At weddings in Tai Tokerau (Northland), the wedding feast is followed by a ceremony known as calling the flowers or the flower ceremony. This evolved when Northland Māori took one aspect of Pākehā wedding ritual – the cutting of the wedding cake – and adapted it for purposes of their own. It has long since become a tradition in its own right.

After the newly married couple have cut the wedding cake, women relatives cut the large bottom tier into substantial pieces, wrap each in a paper serviette and adorn it with an artificial flower, a silver shoe or a horseshoe from the cake. A kaumātua then takes up a central position among the crowd on the marae, a helper holding a platter piled with the wrapped pieces of cake at his side. In a loud voice he calls out the names of the tribes and hapū known to be represented among the guests, beginning with the most remote iwi, moving ever closer to home and ending with the hapū of the marae. As each name is called, a member of that group comes forward to 'claim their flower' that is, the favour-adorned parcel of cake.

Fifty odd years ago, it is said, each 'flower' was claimed by the most senior representative of the group named, and claimants validated their claim by reciting their genealogy, sometimes in competition. Nowadays it is common for older relatives to push children forward to claim the 'flowers', using the ceremony as a way of teaching them their group membership, and claimants usually sing for their flower, choosing anything from an old waiata to an action song or recent popular hit.

Like the pōwhiri, the flower ceremony works to find unity in diversity and to turn strangers into friends. On the one hand, it recognises differences in iwi and hapū membership, reinforcing pride in that membership. On the other hand, because iwi and hapū are characteristic features of Māori culture, it reminds participants of what they have in common, their Māoriness and their common humanity. To make sure that non-Māori do not feel left out, flowers are often called for particular non-Māori guests or for Ngāti Pākehā or Ngāti Tarara (the Dalmatian people). In singing for their flower, guests accept the gift of recognition and friendship symbolised by the flower and help their hosts create a relaxed atmosphere. Typically hosts and visitors end up laughing together.

Modelling a welcome on the flower ceremony

The flower ceremony can be effectively adapted to serve as a welcome ceremony for gatherings attended by representatives of many different groups, whether these are states, ethnic groups, the branches of a large association or

27

independent organisations with common goals. The secret of a successful adaptation lies in the hosts tossing ideas around well beforehand, shaping the ceremony to suit the nature of the gathering, and the setting, and making sure the props are in place. Here is an example devised for a women's conference.

Hosting a Pacific Regional Conference in Auckland in 1972, the New Zealand Federation of University Women decided to open with an adapted version of the flower ceremony, using real flowers. Using a list of the branches attending, the organisers ordered a matching number of small posies with ribbons to tie them to wrists, throats or hair-dos. In pre-conference publicity, each branch was asked to have one representative wearing national dress prepared to speak briefly in the opening ceremony.

The opening session was held in a large raked lecture hall at the university. Delegates took their seats in the body of the hall before the entry of the official party, comprising the members of the national executive, the visiting president of the international federation and the keynote speaker. The president of the New Zealand federation opened proceedings with a speech of welcome to the delegates, introduced the international president, who also spoke, and then handed the microphone to the keynote speaker.

The latter addressed the conference theme of communication across cultural and linguistic boundaries, stressing the importance of non-verbal language and symbolism. She then called the names of the branches attending in alphabetical order. As she named each branch, its representative came forward, received one of the posies from the international president and greeted those attending in her own language and/or English, in words, music or dance, as she chose. After each delegate spoke, she stepped to one side of the rostrum. When the last had spoken, the national executive escorted the international president to the supper room, followed by the representatives who had spoken for their branches and the delegates from the body of the hall, in a light-hearted procession.

THE WORK OF DISCUSSION:
MODES AND GENERAL RULES

The Māori pattern

Discussion in Māori settings is conducted formally, according to unwritten rules. During the welcome ceremony speakers represent their group rather than themselves, follow a pre-arranged order and limit themselves to delivering greetings, providing information about identity and establishing linkages. In contrast, once the welcome is over, all who wish to speak can do so, within the limits set by the modes and rules of discussion.

There are three main ways of organising formal discussion in Māori settings, used at different times for different purposes. Each has advantages and disadvantages.

- haere huri i te whare – going round the (meeting) house, usually beginning at the door with the hosts and proceeding clockwise round the meeting house to end with the most important of the visitors.
- whakawhitiwhiti kōrero – talking criss-cross, in which speakers stand to speak from the places where they are sitting, on both sides of the house, without set order.
- te haere o te rākau – passing the (wooden) stick, a process begun by a host leader, after a short explanation. Objects used for this purpose can include walking sticks and taiaha. Whoever is given the stick must speak and/or sing, in serious or humorous vein, and then hand it on to someone of their choice.

Certain rules apply generally to all three of these discussion modes. The most important are as follows:

- No one person is in charge of managing the discussion. Order is maintained primarily by self-limitation on the part of speakers, and

29

by the kaumātua present, male (koroua) and female (kuia),
sometimes acting independently, sometimes in concert.

- Speakers announce their intention to speak verbally with a phrase
  such as 'Tihe mauri ora!' (The sneeze of life!) or 'Kia hiwa ra!' (Be
  alert!), rise to their feet and speak from a standing position.
- As long as they are standing, speakers hold the floor and are heard
  out without interruption or heckling. They may deal with more than
  one topic in the course of the same speech.
- Not only words but other forms of expression (especially musical
  ones such as waiata and haka) are used by speakers to convey their
  message and by kaumātua to rebuke a rule-breaker, ease tension and
  hostility or revive flagging energies.
- The marae is held to be the appropriate place for voicing grievances
  and disagreements, but also for their mediation and resolution.
  Every effort should be made to resolve problems, and participants
  should leave them behind when they leave the marae.
- Breaches of these rules are dealt with by the oldest and most senior
  kaumātua present. Often it is the women, especially the kuia, who
  calm tense situations. The kaumātua arrange concerted action by
  means of non-verbal communication.

Adapting the Māori pattern for general settings

After formally welcoming participants, it is wise to gather them together in one group for an initial briefing session. Here the facilitators come into their own. Working as a team, supporting and amplifying each other's points, they explain the overall aims of the programme, make sure that participants understand the purpose and parts of the welcome ceremony and set out the general rules and the mode of discussion to be followed in the first session. This should be done as succinctly as possible: participants will learn more by doing than by listening.

If there are more than fifteen participants, now is the time to divide them, or get them to divide themselves, into a series of smaller groups, each with one or preferably two facilitators to provide guidance as necessary.

Whether in plenary or small group sessions the two facilitators work together, taking the lead in turn while the other stands by to comment, criticise and/or put a contrary point of view. Byplay between facilitators helps get across important messages, spoken and unspoken. Māori and Pākehā facilitators working together model the Treaty partnership.

Together the facilitators set out the following general rules:

- Participants sit in a circle with no gaps and nobody sitting outside.
- No one person is in charge or manages the discussion. Participants themselves maintain order and manage conflict by monitoring their own observation of the rules. As a last resort, a facilitator or experienced participant may intervene.
- Intending speakers claim the floor by saying an appropriate phrase and rising to their feet. Whether they remain standing to speak or resume their seats may be decided by consensus or individual preference. Facilitators or participants may suggest appropriate phrases, or these may be left to the inspiration of the moment. They may be in Māori, English or any other language with which the speaker feels comfortable.
- Once a speaker has claimed the floor, interruptions and heckling are outlawed.
- While holding the floor, a speaker may deal with more than one topic, but should be as succinct as possible, knowing when to stop. Self-discipline is the order of the day.

Adopting the Māori emphasis on listening and remembering, organisers should ban tape-recording and note-taking, at least in the early discussion sessions. If participants wish, these could be permitted during explanation and recapitulation sessions or once participants have mastered the skills and want to keep a record for reference purposes.

KŌRERO TAHI: GOING ROUND THE CIRCLE

This method is best used in the first discussion session, immediately after the introductory plenary. It is good for breaking the ice and giving the shy or inhibited an opportunity to speak. Having spoken once, they usually find it easier next time. For best results, the number of participants should be kept to ten or under. Fifteen is possible but beyond that number the group is better divided into smaller ones.

Each group should have two facilitators, though one can cope alone if necessary. It is a good idea for one of the facilitators to begin proceedings or to appoint someone else to do so beforehand, because the first speaker sets a pattern for others to follow. It is especially important that speeches should be short, so that participants do not get bored waiting for their turn. To that end, it is advisable to limit speakers to two or three points. In the first session of the programme, when participants have only just met, this is a good pattern:

- Name, clearly pronounced and repeated so all can hear and remember.
- One or two identifying features the speaker thinks are of key importance about him or herself (for example, ancestry, birthplace, family, special interest).
- One particular topic the speaker wants addressed during discussion.

One of the purposes of this mode of discussion is to help participants to attach names and personalities to faces. Another is to identify the topics and problems participants are most interested in, so that they can be addressed. Instead of working to a pre-set agenda, kōrero tahi proceeds by eliciting the agenda from participants.

Facilitators in particular should develop their capacity for remembering faces, identity markers and topics without the aid of notes, so that they can make sure that none of the topics contributed is overlooked in the subsequent discussion.

KŌRERO TAHI: CRISS-CROSS EXCHANGE

When the process of going round the circle is completed, members of each discussion group move on to the criss-cross exchange mode of discussion. At this point one or both facilitators should briefly review the general rules set out above, with particular stress on the rule against interruptions, then add the following:

- Participants should wait until they have something to contribute to the discussion before signalling that they want to speak.
- Once a speaker has sat down, he or she must refrain from speaking again until several others have spoken, the exact number increasing with the size of the group.
- Speakers are encouraged to voice any resentments or hostilities they are harbouring and to express their feelings honestly. They should, however, avoid immoderate language or personal insults.
- Having voiced their grievances and negative feelings, participants must accept the mediation of others and be willing to negotiate reconciliation, including making or accepting reparation.
- When discussion is over, participants must leave behind any confidential information, grievances or criticisms that have been revealed, carrying away only what is positive and helpful.

These rules are helpful in restraining participants who are dominating, overtalkative or disruptive and in encouraging the shy, inarticulate and un-

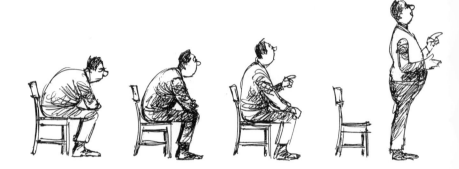

assertive to take part. Even those who are initially hostile to the process cannot resist getting involved when they see how it works. For these reasons, it is particularly important to adhere to the rules against interruption and speaking too often or too long.

Facilitators should wait for and, if necessary, encourage the participants themselves to check breaches of the rules. If lengthy speeches become a problem, the facilitators may ask participants if they wish to set a time limit (for example, five to ten minutes) and how they want to mark time-up. Or they may encourage participants to experiment with other methods of signalling that they have had enough, such as starting a song.

Only when they try observing these rules do many people (both Māori and Pākehā) realise how often they transgress other participants' rights in general discussion. Experience of kōrero tahi often leads Pākehā to revise their previous assessments of Māori colleagues as diffident, ineffectual or lazy, realising for the first time that behaviour they have interpreted in those terms might stem from a different set of values.

If time permits, it is helpful, towards the end of the discussion, to allow participants to share their reactions to the process itself. Be warned: by the end of a session – and especially a day of sessions – using kōrero tahi, participants used to constantly interrupting and talking over others will be frustrated and irritable. They will, however, almost certainly be outnumbered by those grateful for the experience of support and protection from harassment.

Freed from the need to exercise continual control, facilitators should keep a watch on participants' body language, looking particularly for signs that someone is finding is difficult to make or take advantage of openings. If necessary, they may use non-verbal signals to get others to wait till the would-be speaker is ready.

If waiting till someone is ready to speak means that the circle sits in silence for a while, that is not only acceptable but often fruitful. It is far better for speakers to work out what they want to say while others wait than to rise in haste and confuse the debate with poorly considered opinions. Māori acceptance of silence reminds us that it is not a vacuum to be filled with words but is itself a contribution to the debate, as important as rests are in music. Facilitators should watch to see if participants come to appreciate this insight of their own accord and, if they fail to do so, spell it out in so many words.

KŌRERO TAHI: PASSING THE STICK

When discussion using criss-cross exchange has covered the topics raised, or in the evening when people are beginning to lose concentration, it is a good idea to bring participants together again in plenary session and introduce the third discussion mode, passing the stick.

Any suitable object may serve as the stick: a walking stick, a colourful scarf, a broken branch, a book. A facilitator introduces this method by explaining the following rules:

- Everyone to whom the stick is passed must accept it and respond in some way.
- The recipient has complete freedom to choose what to do: share insights from the previous discussion, sing a song, recite a poem, tell a joke.
- After making their contribution, recipients pass the stick on to somebody of their choice, giving their reasons if they wish.
- Once someone has been given the stick, they may take all the time they need to get ready to respond. Others must wait on their readiness.

When the rules have been explained, the facilitator passes the stick to someone who has been briefed to set a model pattern.

This discussion mode is particularly suitable for an evening session, when everyone is tired, as it gives an opportunity to introduce variety and even frivolity. It is also good for use in a closing session, after people have had a chance to get to know each other. I have seen it work very effectively at the end of a conference involving groups from two very different institutions: without being directed, participants kept passing the stick to a member of the other party.

Well handled, this is a good way to give a voice to those shy or anxious people who make a valuable contribution in small groups but retreat into their shells in plenary sessions. When passing the stick to such a person, it is both helpful and kind to throw them a lifeline by suggesting some gift or experience they have to share.

DECISION-MAKING

The Māori pattern

In all discussions intended to reach decisions, Māori aim to achieve consensus, that is, a unified, collective agreement. 'Achieve' is the operative word here: consensus has to be worked for through a process that demands goodwill, patience and freedom from time constraints. In their early speeches, speakers pool all the information they hold relevant to the matter in hand. Then, using whakawhitiwhiti kōrero, they set out a range of different options and scenarios and argue their advantages, disadvantages and likely consequences. Increasingly, as the discussion progresses, they group themselves in support of two or three favoured options, discarding the others. When it becomes obvious that one particular option or compromise between options commands majority support, the holders of minority views let them go (tuku i a ratou) and explicitly assent to the majority view,

so that the final decision may be unanimous. The most respected and senior speaker present articulates this consensus in a final speech, closing the debate.

Adapting the Māori pattern for general settings

Modelled on ngā tikanga Māori, kōrero tahi procedure facilitates the seeking of consensus, but participants must be prepared to invest goodwill, patience and time in order to achieve it. Full consensus is not always possible, because of time constraints and speakers who refuse to abandon minority views. Although extremely desirable, unity is not necessarily the highest good. The group must decide when to continue working towards consensus and when to settle for a majority decision. Often only hindsight can determine whether the holders of minority views were right to give them up for the sake of unity or right to hold to them at its expense.

THE USES OF SONGS AND HUMOUR

The Māori pattern

One of the most striking features of Māori gatherings is the frequency and particular uses made of waiata (songs).

Speakers taking part in the pōwhiri typically conclude their speeches with a waiata: if they do not, listeners will demand one with the call 'Tōu wai! Tōu wai!' [18] The speaker may choose and start the waiata himself, in which case he is joined by other members of his party; or the waiata may be chosen and started by one of the latter, usually a woman. Ideally, the waiata is chosen to extend and complement the content of the speech, but today the choice is often governed by the extent of the singers' repertoire. By standing to sing a waiata for a speaker, the members of his party show their support for him and the sentiments he expresses, while also asserting the mana of their group. The worst thing that can happen to a speaker is to be left to sing alone; this expresses the group's disapproval of his performance and leadership at the expense of the group's mana.

Once the pōwhiri is over, speakers speaking in general discussion may use a well-chosen waiata to drive home a point, to set a mood or bring their

speech to a satisfying conclusion. Men and women with experience and confidence in public settings start a waiata when they see a need, for example, to counter a breach of protocol, to give those expressing strong emotions time to regain control, to lighten a tense atmosphere or to wake people up when they are tired or bored. Women especially use songs to express their views at times when it is inappropriate for them to speak (for example, in the pōwhiri) or when they want to change the course of discussion.

The word waiata covers a very wide range. For older Māori it refers primarily to 'traditional' song-poems composed for particular occasions and sung in unison with a single melodic line, but the term is frequently stretched to cover modern action songs (waiata-a-ringa) and popular songs in both Māori and English. What matters most is that the song chosen is appropriate for the occasion and its intended purpose.

As well as waiata, Māori make effective use of humour to leaven debate and get their points across. Often they combine the two in a comic song. In the not-too-distant past, kuia in particular often delivered their comments in the form of extempore ditties (ruri). Composed on the spot, these made shrewd and humorous comments on personalities, recent happenings and other people's speeches. To this day the most admired speakers convey hard truths in humorous anecdotes and analogies: even their targets can not help laughing, but get the message.

Adapting the Māori pattern for general settings

The Māori insight that discussion does not have to be either limited to the spoken word or invariably solemn is a valuable one. Both music and humour can be used effectively to help participants over rough ground, to mitigate clashes between personalities or strongly held views, to revive flagging energies and recapture wandering attention.

Once the idea of such use is accepted, organisers and participants can work out innovative ways of translating it into action. Songs, especially, provide an opportunity for minority languages to be heard, reminding other participants of their existence, and allow Pākehā to learn more Māori words and acquire the rhythms of the Māori language. Those who have difficulty carrying a tune may find telling a joke or reciting a poem an acceptable alternative to a song.

SUMMING UP – SAYING FAREWELL

The Māori pattern

At hui, discussion on particular topics may be summed up by one or more senior speakers or it may be left hanging in the air to be continued at the next appropriate gathering. The hui as a whole concludes with a farewell ceremony, the poroporoakī.

The poroporoakī is in several ways the reverse of the welcome ceremony. It is as informal as the latter is formal, since hosts and visitors are now on

familiar terms. It takes place not in the sacred space of marae or meeting house but in the dining hall during or after the last meal. The proceedings are begun, not by the hosts, but by the visitors, who announce their coming departure. The roll of speakers is open, not closed: any or all of the visitors may have their say. They thank their hosts for their hospitality, comment on the happenings of the hui and call the workers (the ringa wera or hot hands) from behind the scenes for special appreciation. One or two of the hosts reply, wishing the visitors a safe journey home. The visitors depart, even, if time presses, before the farewell is completed, and the hosts start cleaning up.

Adapting the Māori pattern for general settings

Having brought all the participants together in a final plenary session, the facilitators may invite one person (perhaps the most experienced) to sum up the whole experience, covering method and content, and identifying areas of agreement and disagreement, or they may initiate an open session in which whoever wishes may speak. This is particularly wise at a large conference where relatively few get to speak in plenary as distinct from small group sessions.

When the business of the gathering is concluded, an informally formal farewell makes sound psychological sense. It can be as short or as long as participants like to make it, as serious or as light-hearted. As many participants as wish to may express their thanks to the organisers, to the facilitators of the discussion sessions and to the workers behind the scenes. The hosts respond, speeding them on their way, the visitors depart and the hosts begin to relax.

NOT THE LAST WORD

As explained at the beginning (p.7), the kōrero tahi procedure outlined in this work grew out of numerous experiences of working with Māori partners to facilitate discussion about tikanga Māori and interaction between Māori and Pākehā in Aotearoa New Zealand. Drawing its inspiration from Māori sources, this procedure is, in my experience, gratifyingly successful in helping people from different and even opposing backgrounds work their way through to understanding, reconciliation and friendship. Its effectiveness can be attributed in large part to the emphasis tikanga Māori place on consideration and respect for others and on the flexible adaptation of practice to suit particular contexts. Kōrero tahi is offered to New Zealanders in all their variety as a way of doing partnership as well as talking about it.

NOTES

1. Hoani Waititi grew up in Whangaparaoa in the eastern Bay of Plenty, a member of Te Whānau-ā-Apanui iwi. He trained as a teacher and in 1961 was seconded to the Department of Education to produce Māori language texts for schools. *Te Rangatahi* Volume 1 was published by the Government Printer in 1962, Volume 2 in 1964. In 1963 Hoani was appointed Assistant Officer of Māori Education. He died tragically young in 1965 of leukaemia. His vision and lifework is celebrated on the marae at Whangaparaoa and in the urban marae named after him in West Auckland.

2. Pākehā is a Māori word used by Māori from the early nineteenth century to refer to European visitors and settlers, so different in physical appearance and culture from themselves, ngā tāngata māori (ordinary, familiar people). There are numerous stories about its origin, none authenticated. In present-day usage, its basic reference is to New Zealanders of European descent who are committed citizens of Aotearoa New Zealand, but in appropriate contexts it can be stretched to encompass all non-Māori present, regardless of ethnic origin. The phrase Māori and Pākehā links the two groups referred to as a complementary pair, two halves which together make up the nation.

3. Metge, 1976: 159-60.

4. Metge, 1976: 167-68.

5. Ministerial Advisory Committee 1986.

6. For example, the Children, Young Persons, and Their Families Act 1989 and the Resource Management Act 1991.

7. Metge, 1995: 20-21.

8. The four Māori words in this sentence are all part of the general New Zealand vocabulary, appearing in Orsman (ed.) 1997. Karanga is a ceremonial call of welcome, pōwhiri denotes a ceremonial welcome to a marae, karakia is a prayer and tapu refers to a ritual prohibition or restriction.

9. Orange, 1989; Stenson and Williams, 1990.

10. See fn. 2.

11. Metge and Kinloch, 1978.

12. For a fuller discussion of appreciation not appropriation, see Metge, 1995: 309-12.

13. The doubling of the last two syllables of kōrero (talk) emphasises the reciprocal nature of the talk in discussion.

14. The basic reference of the phrase tāngata whenua is to the group of people (hapū or whānau) recognised as having rights (mana whenua) in a particular locality through inheritance from ancestors and sustained occupation. In this meaning it is contrasted with manuwhiri (visitors) or tauiwi (people from elsewhere). In recent years the term tāngata whenua has been extended to identify the Māori

people in contrast to non-Māori New Zealanders who are identified as Tauiwi. This is a metaphorical usage.

15. Each iwi (tribe) has its own rules governing the spatial disposition of hosts and visitors during the welcome ceremony. The meeting house on a marae represents the body of an ancestor with the gables forming outstretched arms and the head at their apex facing the gateway through which visitors come. In the most common arrangement the hosts occupy seats set out on the marae in front of the right side (te taha matau) of this ancestor/meeting house, the side where the door is located, while visitors take the seats set out opposite, at right angles to or facing the ancestor's left side. Symbolically, the ancestor's right side is the 'strong' side and tāngata whenua sitting on that side are in a position of strength, on their own home ground and spiritual base. Inside the meeting house the hosts usually take the same right side (the left side of someone looking into the house from the doorway!) and visitors go to the ancestor's left side. Among some iwi, the right side of the ancestor is identified as te tara iti, the narrow, door side, and the left as te tara whānui, the wide, window side. This formula emphasises the importance and tapu of the visitors.

16. Pōwhiri means to beckon someone to come on and refers specifically to the welcome chant accompanied by beckoning gestures performed by the hosts as their visitors enter the marae. Use of the term pōwhiri to refer to the *whole* welcome ceremony has come into widespread use in the last two to three decades, but some iwi continue to use other terms. In Tai Tokerau, for example, the welcome ceremony is known as te whakatau or te mihi. Whakatau means to cause to alight and refers to the hauling ashore of the waka in which visitors traditionally arrived. Mihi means to greet and refers specifically to the speeches of greeting. In all three cases, one part of the ceremony is used to signify the whole.

17. The order of speaking is determined by the hosts. Some iwi use the pattern called paeke in which the host speakers speak first in a block, followed by the guest speakers in a matching block. Other iwi use the tūmai, tūatu procedure (also called utuutu) in which tāngata whenua and manuwhiri speakers alternate, beginning and concluding with the tāngata whenua.

13. 'Tou wai!' (Your wai!) involves a play on words. Wai is at once an abbreviated form of waiata and the word for water, which in Māori thinking is closely associated with and an apt symbol for the gift of life.

REFERENCES AND READING LIST

Durie, Mason. 'Marae and Implications for a Modern Māori Psychology', *Journal of the Polynesian Society*, Vol. 108 (4), 1999.

Harawira, Wena. *Te Kawa o te Marae: A guide for all marae visitors*, Auckland, Reed, 1997.

Lancaster, Diana. *Wars of Welcome: What's going on when Māori meet?*, Whitianga, Hattie Bee Lines, 1993.

Metge, Joan. *The Māoris of New Zealand: Rautahi*, London, Routledge & Kegan Paul, 1976, Chapters 15 and 16.

Metge, Joan and Patricia Kinloch. *Talking Past Each Other: Problems of Cross Cultural Communication*, Wellington, Victoria University Press, 1978.

Metge, Joan. *New Growth From Old: The Whanau in the Modern World*, Wellington, Victoria University Press, 1995, Chapter 13.

Ministerial Advisory Committee on a Māori Perspective for the Department of Social Welfare *Puao-Te-Ata-Tu (Daybreak)*, with *Appendix to Puao-Te-Ata-Tu*, Wellington, Government Printer, 1986.

Orange, Claudia. *The Story of a Treaty*, Wellington, Allen & Unwin in association with the Port Nicholson Press, 1989.

Orsman, H W. *The Dictionary of New Zealand English*, Auckland, Oxford University Press, 1997.

Salmond, Anne. *Hui: A Study of Māori Ceremonial Gatherings*, Wellington, Reed, 1975.

Stenson, Marcia and Tu Williams. *The Treaty of Waitangi*, Auckland, Addison Wesley Longman, 1990.

Tauroa, Pat and Hiwi. *Te Marae: A Guide to Customs and Protocol*, Auckland, Reed, 1986.

KŌRERO TAHI : GUIDELINES FOR FACILITATORS
WORKING WITH SMALL GROUPS

When introducing participants to kōrero tahi, it is a good idea if two facilitators can work together, but one can work alone if need be. Once participants are familiar with the rules, they may either take it in turns to act as facilitator(s) or dispense with that role altogether.

Facilitators should never forget that their role is to *facilitate*, that is, make it easier for the group to achieve the goals of the discussion. Once they have explained the rules, the less the facilitators have to say, the better.

1. Seat participants in a circle with no gaps.

2. At the first meeting only, stand to welcome participants; wait for or, if necessary, prime someone to respond.

3. Explain the basics of kōrero tahi as briefly as possible, making the following points:
    *   Kōrero tahi draws on tikanga Māori as source.
    *   Responsibility for managing the discussion rests with the group as a whole: no one person is in charge. Each group member is responsible for monitoring his/her own observation of the rules.
    *   Intending speakers rise to their feet saying an appropriate phrase and thereby claim the floor. They may remain standing or sit down to speak.
    *   Once a speaker has claimed the floor, he/she must not be interrupted.
    *   Speakers should not rise to speak until sure they have something to say.
    *   If no one is ready to speak, participants wait in silence till someone rises to his/her feet.

4. Initiate discussion by going round the circle, asking each person to contribute three items, briefly:
    *   his/her name, clearly pronounced;
    *   a significant identifying feature about himself or herself;
    *   the topic(s) he/she wants to have discussed.
    Prime a group member to begin the process, setting a suitably brief pattern. The topics contributed become the *agenda for discussion*. After the initial meeting of a group, the first two items are dropped and going round the circle is used simply to set the agenda.

5. When everyone has spoken and the agenda has been set, introduce criss-cross exchange, briefly setting out the following, additional rules:
   - Group members speak when they wish to, from where they are sitting.
   - Speakers may deal with more than one topic but should do so succinctly, placing time limits on themselves.
   - Once a speaker has sat down, he/she must refrain from speaking again until at least two or three others have spoken.
   - Before rising to their feet, speakers should check to see if someone else wishes to speak, defer to others and encourage the diffident.
   - Speakers are encouraged to voice grievances and hostilities. It is acceptable to express strong emotion but personal insults should be avoided if possible.
   - Having expressed themselves strongly, group members should accept the mediation of others and negotiate reconciliation.
   - When the session is over, group members must leave confidential information, grievances and criticisms behind.

6. In a later session facilitators might use the alternative procedure of passing the stick, using any object as the stick. The facilitator explains that whoever holds the stick chooses who to pass it on to; the recipient must respond but may choose whether to make a speech, tell a story, sing a song, etc. The facilitator then passes the stick to his/her own choice.

7. At the last session the facilitators reserve the last fifteen minutes for group members to say thank you and farewell to each other.

TALKING ABOUT PARTNERSHIP

When people of different backgrounds come together to know each other better, sort out differences and plan a common enterprise, it can be helpful to begin by directing their attention away from their particular shared history with its problems and mistakes and set them to thinking about such key concepts as cooperation and partnership. The word partnership in particular is often used, for example in relation to the Treaty of Waitangi, but is commonly the focus of much talking past each other, because speakers read their own assumptions into the concept without checking to see if they are shared and without fully exploring its implications. Some people have advocated dropping the idea of partnership in favour of cooperation, as a more general and neutral term.

Kōrero tahi procedure can be usefully employed to explore these concepts, either in a meeting arranged for the purpose or in the context of a larger gathering. Here is a suggested pattern for the conduct of such a discussion.

- After welcoming participants, the facilitators explain the kōrero tahi procedure and divide participants into small groups, each with a facilitator of its own.

- In each group the facilitator begins the process of going round the circle, asking participants to give their names and any information they think relevant about themselves (ethnicity, iwi, place of origin or residence etc.).

- The facilitator asks all members to think of a partnership, either good or bad, and tell the group about it when they are ready, using the rules of criss-cross exchange. This process should produce a variety of partnerships (in work situations, marriage, sport, dancing etc.) involving any number of parties of both equal and unequal standing.

- The facilitator divides a large sheet of paper into two columns headed with plus and minus signs. After each story, group members identify the feature(s) that enable them to characterise the partnership as good or bad and enter these in the relevant column. Restrict the number of features drawn from each story to one or two so that everyone has a chance to contribute. The recurrence of a feature can be marked with a tick.

- It is important that participants draw the ideas out of their own experience. The facilitator should compose his or her own list of possible features beforehand but use this only as a checklist to make sure that something important is not overlooked. The issue of power-sharing is the most important of all and needs to be highlighted.

- Reviewing the entries they have made and rewording and reordering them as necessary, each group draws up a list of the features essential to a good partnership to hang on the wall.

- The groups can then proceed, if they choose, to discuss broader questions, for example, the differences and similarities between the concepts of partnership and cooperation, and the usefulness of these terms in discussions about the Treaty of Waitangi and national and local relations between Māori and Pākehā.

- If participants have been divided into small groups, they should be brought back together in a plenary session. Each group might be asked to share one or two of the best stories contributed and/or their ideas on the broader issues. The 'essential features of a good partnership' could be hung round the walls of the main meeting place.